LEVERS

Louise Spilsbury

New York

Published in 2019 by The Rosen Publishing Group
29 East 21st Street, New York, NY 10010

Copyright © 2019 by The Rosen Publishing Group

Produced for Rosen by Calcium Creative Ltd
Editors for Calcium Creative Ltd: Sarah Eason and Harriet McGregor
Designer: Paul Myerscough
Picture researcher: Rachel Blount

Illustration by Geoff Ward

Picture credits: Cover: Shutterstock: Zurijeta; Inside: Shutterstock: Julia Albul: p. 7; Wang An Qi: p. 29; Anna G: p. 19; Asia Images Group: p. 20; Axpitel: p. 25; Rob Bayer: p. 27t; Corepics VOF: pp. 8–9; DarioZg: p. 22; Defotoberg: p. 21; Goodluz: pp. 1, 16; Imfoto: p. 18; Evgeniy Kalinovskiy: pp. 26–27; Tidarat Kamonmaitreechit: p. 23; Kzenon: p. 9t; Pavel L Photo and Video: p. 4; Ponsulak: p. 24; Pryzmat: p. 5; Catalin Rusnac: p. 13; K Satdamrong: pp. 14–15; Schankz: p. 10; Viorel Sima: p. 11; Dimitar Sotirov: p. 12; Stockphoto Mania: p. 28; T. Den: pp. 3, 17; Zynatis: p. 15t.

Cataloging-in-Publication Data

Names: Spilsbury, Louise.
Title: Levers / Louise Spilsbury.
Description: New York : PowerKids Press, 2019. | Series: Technology in action | Includes glossary and index.
Identifiers: LCCN ISBN 9781538337547 (pbk.) | ISBN 9781538337530 (library bound) | ISBN 9781538337554 (6 pack)
Subjects: LCSH: Levers--Juvenile literature.
Classification: LCC TJ147.S67 2019 | DDC 621.8'11--dc23

Manufactured in the United States of America

CPSIA Compliance Information: Batch CSPK18: For further information, contact Rosen Publishing, New York, New York, at 1-800-237-9932.

Contents

Machines and Forces

Every day, we use different machines to help us do many different things. Machines help us do **work**, such as lifting and moving objects.

Work and Forces

For scientists, work means using **force** to move an object. A force is a push or a pull. We use force whenever we move an object from one place to another. We use force to carry a bag of books or clean a car. We even use force to turn the page of a book. We use more force to move a heavy object than a light object, or to move an object a long distance instead of a short distance.

A diving board is a type of lever. It helps a diver jump into the air with more force.

Machines in Action

Machines can change the strength or **direction** of a force. This makes work easier or faster. Some machines are simple, such as scissors and axes. Some are more complex, such as cars and computers. There are six types of simple machines: the inclined plane, the wedge, the screw, the lever, the wheel and axle, and the pulley. Let's take a look at some simple machines in action: levers.

This simple machine is a crowbar. It is a lever and it pulls nails out of wood.

Parts of a Lever

A lever is simple machine with only two working parts. These parts are called the **arm** and the **fulcrum**. Scissors, bottle openers, and a human arm are all levers.

Arm and Fulcrum

A lever's arm is a straight, hard object such as a board or a rod. The user pushes or pulls the arm. A lever always turns or balances on one point. This point is called the fulcrum. The object moved by the lever is the **load**. The **effort** is the force needed to operate any simple machine. To operate a lever, effort is applied to the arm.

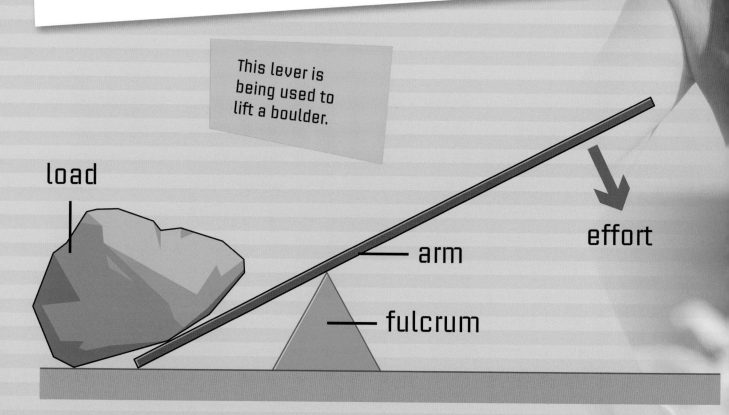

This lever is being used to lift a boulder.

load

arm

fulcrum

effort

How Levers Work

Imagine a ruler lying across a pencil. The ruler is the arm and the fulcrum is the point that touches the pencil. If you push down on one end of the ruler, the other end moves up. If you place a load, such as an eraser, on one end of the ruler and press down on the opposite end, you lift the eraser. Your effort is called the **input force**. The lift at the other end is the **output force**. The farther the input force is from the fulcrum, the easier the load is to lift. Let's take a look at levers in action!

When you lift an object, your arm is the lever arm and your elbow is the fulcrum.

arm

load

fulcrum

See technology in action!

Technology in Action:
Levers at Work

Let's take a look at oars as levers.

The rower pulls the oars. This is the input force. The oars **pivot**, or turn, on the fulcrum.

The places where the oars rest in their brackets are the fulcrum points.

CLOSE TO THE ACTION

In this **canoe**, the rower holds one oar in two places. The top hand holds the oar loosely and keeps still. This is the fulcrum. The lower hand provides the input force and moves the oar, which is the arm.

The oars are the arms.

The output force pushes on the water. The water is the load. The force makes the boat move through the water.

First-Class Levers

There are different types of levers: first class, second class, and third class. **First-class levers** are the most common.

How First-Class Levers Work

In a first-class lever, the load and the effort are on opposite sides of the fulcrum. The fulcrum, the fixed point against which the lever turns, is located between the input force and the output force. It supports the arm and the load. When effort is applied to one side of the arm in one direction, it causes the lever to pivot about the fulcrum, producing an output force in the opposite direction.

Scissors are two first-class levers joined at the fulcrum.

When you nod your head down, your head and neck work like a first-class lever. The fulcrum is your neck, the load is your head, and the effort is the neck and shoulder muscles pulling down.

Different First-Class Levers

There are a lot of examples of first-class levers: seesaws (or teeter-totters), crowbars, can openers, oars, bottle openers, bicycle hand brakes, **hammers** (when the claw end is used to pull out a nail), and shoehorns. These levers have only one arm. But some first-class levers have two arms, such as scissors.

Levers and Balance

To lift a load using a lever, it works best if the fulcrum is close to the load. Then, distance from the input force to the fulcrum is longer than the distance from the load to the fulcrum. We push down on the arm and lift the load. However, levers can also be used to balance loads.

Balancing Loads

A **balancing lever** is a first-class lever with the load and the input force on opposite sides of a fulcrum. A set of balance scales is a balancing lever. Weights are added to one side of the lever. Goods are added to the other end of the lever until the arm is level and the lever is balanced.

fulcrum

In this balance scale, the fulcrum is at the midpoint between the two ends of the lever arm.

Unbalancing Loads

In ancient times, soldiers developed a weapon called a trebuchet. This was a first-class lever. A long arm was positioned on a frame so that it could pivot. A rock was placed in a sling on the long end of the arm. When a force was applied to the short end, it propelled the rock through the air toward the enemy. Let's take a look at balancing levers in action.

load

lever arm

fulcrum

The trebuchet was like a giant catapult and it could be a deadly weapon.

input force

See technology in action!

Technology in Action:
Balancing Levers

Let's take a look at the
technology in action on a seesaw.

The fulcrum of a seesaw is in
the center of the lever arm.

The lever arm
is balanced
and level.

CLOSE TO THE ACTION

If an adult and a child sit on a seesaw, the difference in weights unbalances the seesaw. The heavier end sinks and the lighter end lifts. To make the seesaw work, the adult must push their feet hard against the ground. This creates a force that is strong enough to lift his or her own weight, and bring the other end of the seesaw down.

If the children at the each end of the seesaw weigh the same, the input force and the output force are equal and balanced.

Second-Class Levers

All levers have an arm, a fulcrum, and a load. The input force is always positioned somewhere on the lever arm. In each class of levers, the position of the fulcrum, the load, and the input force changes.

It only takes a small input force to pull up on the wheelbarrow handles and lift the load inside.

load

fulcrum

arm

How Second-Class Levers Work

In a **second-class lever**, the load and the input force are on the same side of the fulcrum. The load is between the fulcrum and the input force. So, the input force is at one end of the arm, the output force happens in the middle of the arm, and the fulcrum is at the opposite end of the arm.

All Sorts of Second-Class Levers

Second-class levers are used in many devices including wheelbarrows, nutcrackers, bottle openers, doors with **hinges**, and staplers. A wheelbarrow may not look like a lever, but think about how it works. We lift the handles (input force). The lever arm is the handles and frame of the wheelbarrow. The load sits in the bucket, and the wheel is the fulcrum.

load

arm

fulcrum

This ballerina is using a second-class lever. Her toes are the fulcrum, her foot is the lever arm, and her calf muscles provide the effort to lift the load (her body).

A Helping Hand

Levers that are first or second class always give us a **mechanical advantage**. A mechanical advantage is when a simple machine makes a small push or pull into a much larger push or pull.

This car is being lifted using a long lever attached to a jack, which is a device that raises the car. The longer the lever, the easier it is to lift an object.

load

arm

fulcrum

18

fulcrum

load

input force

How It Works

A lever changes a small input force into a greater output force. This means that it takes less effort to lift a load. This mechanical advantage makes lifting the load seem to be an easier task. In fact, the overall amount of work done is the same. To make the effort less, you must move a greater distance.

The Trade-Off

A lever helps us trade effort for distance. To lift a load with half the effort, the distance from the fulcrum to the input force must be twice the distance between the load and the fulcrum. So, to cut the effort of lifting up a load by 1 foot (30 cm) from a fulcrum in half, you would need to apply a force 2 feet (60 cm) from the fulcrum. Let's take a look at levers in action.

When you squeeze the two arms of a nutcracker, the levers multiply your input force by about four times. This allows you to crack open a nut easily.

See technology in action!

Technology in Action:
Mechanical Advantage

Let's take a look at the technology in action on the doors of this sports car.

CLOSE TO THE ACTION

Most car doors open outward. The hinge is the fulcrum and the input force is applied to the handle. The load, the weight of the door, is at the center of the lever. Imagine trying to open the door by pushing near the hinge (fulcrum). It would be very difficult.

Falcon-wing doors open upward instead of outward.

The lever arm is the car door.

We apply the input force to the handle.

The load is the door itself.

The hinges are fixed to the edge of the roof. The hinge is the fulcrum.

Third-Class Levers

Third-class levers are a little different from those of first or second class. First- and second-class levers give us a mechanical advantage. They make our pushes and pulls stronger. Third-class levers require a large input force to move a small load. So why do we use them?

How Do They Work?

Third-class levers have the fulcrum at one end and the load at the other end. The input force is between the load and the fulcrum. The effort is greater than the load. This makes third-class levers such as tweezers, chopsticks, and barbecue tongs very useful for picking up things that are small or hot, or that could be squashed or broken under a large force.

With a third-class lever such as a baseball bat, the player applies a larger force so that he or she only has to move his or her hands a short distance.

lever arm

fulcrum

load

effort

Going Farther

The other advantage of third-class levers is that because a larger force is used, the load travels a greater distance. A baseball bat is a third-class lever. The end of the bat in the player's hands is the fulcrum. The baseball that they hit is the load. Swinging the bat makes the ball fly into the air. Tennis rackets and cricket bats are also third-class levers that can be used to hit balls a long distance.

Compound Levers

Some machines contain more than one lever. These can be the same type of lever, or they can contain different types of levers. When more than one lever is combined to make a machine, we call it a **compound lever**.

How It Works

In a compound lever, two or more levers are connected together. The arm of one lever can link to the arm of another lever. In this type of machine, the load of one lever becomes the effort applied to another lever.

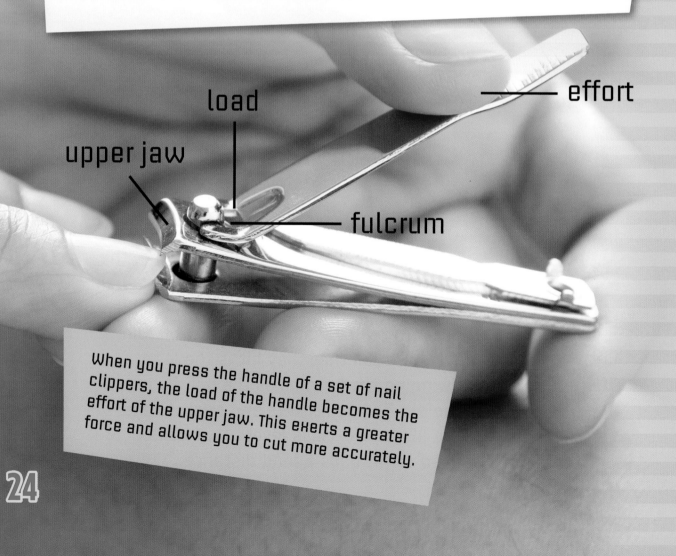

load

effort

upper jaw

fulcrum

When you press the handle of a set of nail clippers, the load of the handle becomes the effort of the upper jaw. This exerts a greater force and allows you to cut more accurately.

Playing a piano uses many levers. Pushing a piano key operates a set of levers that make a hammer strike a string. The string creates a sound.

Using Compound Levers

A nail clipper is a compound lever. It is made up of a second- and third-class lever joined together. The handle is a second-class lever. The clipping part is a third-class lever. We use a compound lever to gain a mechanical advantage or to operate in a limited space. In the nail clipper, the output force of the second-class lever is used as the input force for the third-class lever. Let's take a look at compound levers in action.

See technology in action!

Technology in Action:
Compound Levers

Let's take a look at the technology in action on these powerful bolt cutters.

A bolt cutter is a compound lever.

The handles are two large first-class levers.

The effort of pressing on the long handles produces a large load. This load becomes the input force (effort) that moves the blades.

CLOSE TO THE ACTION

Bolt cutters can slice through thick steel with ease. The mechanical advantage of bolt cutters increases the input force by about 36 times. Moving the handles by 3 feet [1 m] using 56 pounds [25 kg] of force moves the blades 1 inch [2.5 cm], but with a cutting force of 2,000 pounds [907 kg]!

Two extra pivot points link the pairs of levers together. This increases the mechanical advantage even more.

The blades are two small first-class levers.

Life with Levers

People have been using levers for thousands of years. In the past, people used levers for moving heavy stones or for digging. Tools such as **hoes**, slings, and oars are all levers and were invented and used long ago. They are still used today.

Many Uses

Levers are used in many machines. They change the output force or the distance over which a force acts. On a bicycle, for example, the brakes are a system of levers. To work them, the rider pulls on a handle that is a lever. Doing this operates a pivoting lever that pulls the brake cables tight. It makes rubber pads grip the wheel and slow its movement.

brake levers

This rider is pulling back on the brake levers to slow down.

Mighty Machines

Some of the biggest and mightiest levers in the world are the tower cranes found at construction sites. The long arm of a tower crane is called a boom. A tower crane is usually a first class lever. The boom has a heavy **counterweight** at one end to keep it from falling over when the opposite end lifts a heavy load. Levers are in action all around us. Our world would be a very different place without them!

fulcrum

counterweight

boom

tower

The load can be lifted at the opposite end of the boom from the counterweight. The effort is made by the motor.

Glossary

arm A long, rigid part of a lever.

balancing lever A weighing device in which the fulcrum is in the middle of the arm.

canoe A light, narrow boat with pointed ends.

compound lever A system of two or more levers. The force from one lever is transferred to and operates the other lever or levers.

counterweight A heavy weight that balances a machine.

direction The path or line along which something moves or faces.

effort The force used to move something.

first-class levers Levers in which the fulcrum is located between the input force and the load.

force A push or a pull.

fulcrum A point or object on which a lever rests and rotates (also known as a pivot).

hammers Bars with a heavy head used to hit something or to act as a lever and remove a nail.

hinges Movable joints that allow part of a machine to pivot.

hoes Long-handled gardening tools with a thin blade at one end.

input force The amount of force used to operate a simple machine.

load A force or weight a machine moves or produces.

mechanical advantage The increase of output force relative to input force.

output force The amount of force produced using a simple machine.

pivot To turn about a fixed point.

second-class lever A lever in which the fulcrum is located at one end of the lever arm. The load is between the input force and the fulcrum.

third-class levers Levers in which the fulcrum is located at one end of the lever arm. The input force is between the load and the fulcrum.

work The force needed to move an object.

Further Reading

BOOKS

Coutts, Lyn. *Machines*. Hauppauge, NY: Barron's Educational Series, 2017.

Miller, Tim, and Rebecca Sjonger. *Levers in My Makerspace*. New York, NY: Crabtree Publishing Company, 2017.

Rivera, Andrea. *Levers*. Minneapolis, MN: Abdo Zoom, 2017.

Rustad, Martha E. H. *Levers*. North Mankato, MN: Capstone Press, 2018.

Weakland, Mark. *Fred Flintstone's Adventures with Levers*. North Mankato, MN: Capstone Press, 2016.

WEBSITES

Due to the changing nature of Internet links, PowerKids Press has developed an online list of websites related to the subject of this book. This site is updated regularly. Please use this link to access the list: www.powerkidslinks.com/tia/levers

Index